The Empty Palace

Tony Bradman • Jonatronix

Max's mission log

Cat, Ant, Tiger and I have made some new micro-friends … an alien called Nok and his robot, Seven!

Together, we travelled through space on board the micro-ship Excelsa to Nok's home, Planet Exis.

When we got there, we found that Planet Exis had been taken over by a space villain called Badlaw and his army of robotic Krools. Now, Nok wants our help to defeat Badlaw!

Current location: Planet Exis

In our last adventure ...

We set off through the Exian forest to find Nok's parents. Nok told us that Badlaw is stealing the planet's power.

A swarm of insects called buzzles chased us.

The buzzles didn't hurt us. They just wanted some of Nok's power to make them feel better.

The friends had just reached the edge of the forest. In front of them was a magnificent building with tall glass windows.

"Home!" cried Nok. He ran towards a door at the front of the building. "Wow!" said Tiger. "What a place!"

The others hurried after Nok. They walked into a huge entrance hall.

"This is amazing," said Cat, looking around in wonder.

"Well, it is the royal palace," said Seven.

"Nok lives in a *palace?*" said Max.

"Of course," said Seven. "He is a prince. His parents are the king and queen of Exis."

"He's a prince?" said Ant.

"He didn't tell us!" said Tiger.

They headed deeper inside the palace. It was very quiet.

"Where is everybody?" asked Tiger.

"I don't know. It is usually really busy," said Seven. "We had better find Nok."

They entered a vast room. Nok was sitting in front of two empty thrones. He had his head in his hands.

"My parents are missing!" he sobbed.

"Don't worry, Nok," said Cat. "I'm sure they're OK."

"Hey, what's this?" asked Ant. He picked up a thin, metal object that was on one of the thrones.

"It's a message tablet," said Seven.

Just then, a hologram formed in front of them. It was a recorded message from Badlaw.

"I have the king and queen. I won't release them until you give me *the map*!"

"What's he talking about, Nok?" asked Max. "What map?"

Before Nok could answer, Tiger's watch started flashing red. It meant there was danger nearby.

"Oh, no," said Tiger. "Krool alert!"

Suddenly there was a loud explosion. The door to the throne room burst into a thousand pieces. In rolled a Krool.

The Krool split apart like segments of an orange. Metallic legs and arms grew out of its body.

"Let's get out of here!" yelled Tiger.

"Don't panic," said Max. He turned to the Krool. "We're not scared," he said. "There are six of us but only one of you!"

At that moment, four more Krools rolled into the room.

"Uh, oh!" said Ant.

"Run!" shouted Max.

Nok led the way through a door at the back of the throne room. They ran down a hallway.

The Krools sped after them, bouncing off the walls.

The friends came to another door. They ran out of the palace and back into the forest.

"This way!" said Nok, heading up a narrow path.

They came to a clearing and stopped. "Did we lose them?" asked Tiger, panting. Cat looked behind them. "I don't think so ..." she said.

The Krools rolled in from different directions.

"We're surrounded!" said Tiger.

"On the count of three SHRINK!" said Max. "One ... two ... three ..."

The friends shrank and dived out of the way. The Krools were going too fast to stop. They crashed into each other with a *BANG!* Sparks flew. They burst apart in a tangle of twisted metal.

The friends grew back to normal size.
"That showed them!" said Tiger.

Only Nok looked sad. "Badlaw still has my parents," he said.

"We need to find out about this map," said Cat. "Is there anyone who can help us?"

"Yes," said Nok. "His name is Arkon. We also call him *The Old One.*"

"Where can we find him?" asked Tiger.

Before Nok could speak, the friends were surrounded by a blue glow ...

Seconds later, they found themselves in front of a strange figure in a blue robe. "You do not find The Old One," Arkon said. "*He finds you.* Welcome to the Pool of Power."

Find out what happens next in *Battle with the Beast.*